To render the ordinary and the everyday extraordinary, suspended, luminous…Roe's work was making me feel this. It reminded me of the E.B. White quote about loving the world.

-Playwright Nancy Bell

Kerri J. Roe's poetry reminds me of my favorite things about Mary Oliver, how she zeroes in on a specific aspect of nature, and then slowly zooms out, coaxing the human out of nature and nature out of the human.

-Poet SethWilson Gray

This poetry is REAL, and that always reminds me of what actually matters, so I can let go of what doesn't.

-Poet K. Lorentzen

my heart walks
in pieces

my heart walks in pieces

poems

by Kerri J. Roe

my heart walks in pieces: poems
Copyright © 2024 by Kerri J. Roe

All rights reserved. No part of this publication may be reproduced, distributed, or transmitted in any form or by any means, including photocopying, recording, or other electronic or mechanical methods, without the prior written permission of the publisher, excepts in the case of brief quotations embedded in critical reviews and certain other noncommercial uses permitted by copyright law. For permission requests, write to the publisher at the address below.

Without limiting the author's and publisher's exclusive rights, any unauthorized use of this publication to train generative Artificial Intelligence (AI) is expressly prohibited.

ISBN: 979-8-9917218-0-6 (Paperback)
ISBN: 979-8-9917218-1-3 (eBook)

Library of Congress Control Number: 2024923953

Any references to historical events, real people, or real places are used fictitiously. Names, characters, and places are products of the author's imagination.

Cover art and book design © 2024 by Kerri J. Roe

First printing edition 2024.

Quillflower Creative, LLC
PO Box 1281
Kenai, AK 99669

Printed in the USA.

Visit the author's website at www.kerrijroe.com

For my children,
who carry all the best pieces
of my heart within them.

CONTENTS

Living
Deciduous 3
Elemental 4
Composition 5
Seasoned 6
Precipitous 7
Drops Of Time 8
After The Swan 10
From The Ashes 12
The Edge Of Snow 13
Romancing The Soul 14
Tesserae 16
Nebula 17
This Isn't Going To Work 18
Regrets 19
Batten Down 20
Overlook 21
Untitled 22
Icebound 23

Losing
Riding The Rails 27
Prison Break 30
Awakening 32
Nocturne's Spell 34

Beauty In the Dying 36
Limbo 38
That Moment 39
Sylvan Shower 40
G[r]o[w]ing 41
Passage 42
Dreamscape 44
Moonshine 45
Epitaph 46

<u>Breathing</u>
Metamorphosis 49
My Heart Walks in Pieces 50
Le Café 52
Vignette 53
River 54
On the Backs of Waves 55
The Artist 56
Reflections 57
A Legacy in Crystal 58
Sway 60
Apini 62
Bounty 63
Gossamer 64
Water, Living 66
Oculus 67
That Thing with Feathers 68
Breathe 70

Living

Deciduous

Is this, then, the autumn of my life,
the seeds
I've carried
scattered across the Earth,
my branches skeletal, bare
to the frost and cold?
Still I stand, a
narrow stubbornness
against the elements, a
statement of wistful
defiance against the
building bitterness.

I wish for my seeds
rich soil in which to dig their roots
nourishing rains to sustain them
warm sunshine to draw their faces
to the sky, forever stretching
toward the light
mild winters of rest and peaceful
reminiscence
and communal root systems
to keep them together
in the darkness.

I drop my vibrant leaves
tears of copper and gold and
scarlet
I hope you will see their beauty
and think softly of me.

Kerri J. Roe

Elemental

water   calls my name
    the undersides of waves
          clarity
  the foam illusory
              soft to touch
the violence   of the whitecaps
      clashing in battle
   the changing   of the tide a
      moving boundary
  a million shades to tease
     the eye
    blues, greys, greens   flecked
     with silver light
  the peace   of unconquerable
      ferocity
teasing the shore   with its
     siren call
  my soul   gasping, straining
      to answer

Composition

Chords lift from the keys,
Pianist's foot keeps time
Like a bionic metronome.
The small table holds
A cup o' tea, a cup o' soup
And my lap holds the paper;
Pencil twirls across its stage
And I have a moment
Of feeling Hemingway-ish
In some Parisian café,
Using my few francs
To buy a space in
Some artsy district corner
To open the doors

To the words
Building like a flood
Behind the nondescript walls
Of my body,
The spilling of my thoughts
And the crashing waves of my muse
Finding release in graphite
Flung across a page;

And the peace
Slides its way down my limbs
Following in the wake
Of this undammable tide.

Kerri J. Roe

Seasoned

Azure onion dome
weathered white steeple
cracked with decades of
rain, and snow, and sun,
and canons of orthodoxy

Wooden shingles now gray
lap-sided roof peaks
framing windows that once
gave escape to
prayers and
voices of hope and
rites and recitations
and love and loss

Generations instinctively
echoing the requests
of those who came before,
for harvest, and home,
for comfort, and peace,
The words ingrained
in the soul
of the wood.

Precipitous

Sing me your lullaby
dancing on a tin roof
pattering and pounding
in soothing rhythm

Tell me your verses
of evaporated hopes
gatherings of condensation
and falling in a new land

Whisper my name
in ripples on placid waters
in chatterings of dripping eaves
and kisses on shivering petals

Grant me sweet release
cleansing my tangled mind
sliding on moon-white skin
seducing with liquid touch

Kerri J. Roe

Drops Of Time

It's those little things
The ones that pass so quickly
The moments that make us stop,
  Pause,
Breathe again
The ones we wished
  We'd held onto
The thick, honey-sweet beauty
Glistening in the passage of time
Shining like sunset rays
On tidal waters
Startlingly beautiful
Momentarily grasped
Too soon past

The love that lifts,
The fall, the burn,
  The crash
The joy that holds,
The squalls abided,

My Heart Walks in Pieces

Struggles withstood
The imperfections
Marking the perfection
Of a real, unimagined life
Too true to be false
Too messy for the fairy tale
Too fleeting, then lost
Too wondrous to be forgot.

Kerri J. Roe

After The Swan
(Swan Lake Fire 2019)

Crosshatch in
    charcoal shades
  ashy husks and
    impenetrable blacks
in tangles on scorched earth;
  ebony spires
standing in stark monument
to a life lived in
    lush overgrowth –
Musical balls in
palaces of birch and spruce
    and cottonwood greens
  whispered trysts among
    the alders
  and laughing leaf races
on brook-ish trails

My Heart Walks in Pieces

The subdued commotion
   of sylvan soiree

Now silent,
the scent of smoke
   a lingering memento of
that which was,

and the curling green
    of newborn shoot

a promise of what will be.

Kerri J. Roe

From The Ashes

Wispy tendrils wind their way up into the
    air
  smoke rising from cooling
              ash
  gray-white-black collapsing in
onto gleaming red-orange
    windows to fluorescent opulence
  quickly shuttered by chemical reaction
      seemingly molecular
  changes
    covering the heat within
masquerading as a diminished thing
      its heart buried in what's been
                burnt
    stirred by the faintest breeze
  bits of past's debris teased away
    swirling, gliding, winging on scalloped
    ringlets of misty dreams
      rekindled.

The Edge Of Snow

Ice edges its way
stealthily along the shore
Stretching fingers of
broken-glass crystals
and frozen-summer dreams
As leaves of grass don
furry frosty coats
Birch's burnt-orange teardrops
crunching beneath
wool-clad feet
Mocking clouds float
on vaporous exhale
Cold burning the lining
of nostrils and
Summer's bedchamber
As seasons pirouette
In fathomless beauty
and immeasurably lucid harmony
on the stage of
Gaia's heart

Kerri J. Roe

Romancing The Soul

Trails of adventure
Call to open hearts
Irresistible allure
To wanderer
And poet alike

Mountaintops and canyons
Hidden lakes and
Secret islands
Guarded by
Midnight bruins

Palmed antlers
Throwing shadows
Among white birch and
Gray-green cottonwood
And floating eagle nests

Chimes of dancing ice
On wind-feathered waters
Singing requiem
A melting concerto at
Winter's last revel

My Heart Walks in Pieces

Echoes of ancient glaciers
Reminders of Khione's
Charming tyranny
Terra's rumblings
And Creator's dream

Vistas of impossible perfection
Glimpses of heaven
Glimpses
of the depths
of our hearts
of our souls

Kerri J. Roe

Tesserae

Hold my heart
hold it gently and with great care
Hold the pieces
with open grasp
Careful lest the fragments
cut you
with their brokenness
Watch the light glint
off the edges
Glimpses of beauty

in the shards
Recognize
the strength in
the shattering
the hope found in

disrepair
the wisdom in
the cracks
the magnificence of
our remnants

the brilliant mosaic of
our coming together

Nebula

Worlds lie behind her eyes
Galaxies of unexplored beauty
Tragedies and comedies
And whole long lives
Hopes and dreams
Endless loves and broken hearts
Landscapes lit by
Impossible light
Oceans of longings
Fed by Elysian rivers
Mountains flung against

Preternatural skies
Craggy peaks lined by
Vales and valleys half-seen
Traced by mists
Depths indiscernible
To naked eye
Breadth and width
Only to be discovered
By the most dedicated of souls

Kerri J. Roe

This Isn't Going To Work

"Yeah," she says,
"I got it,"
As the black hole
Opens wide
With its visceral pull
Like a painfully
Deep yawn
That never quite
Completes; then
She strengthens
Her spine, and
Looks him in the eye,
And walks away
With her head high,
Crumbling inside.

Regrets

Regrets is too harsh a word,
and the wrong idea anyway.
There is a smile on the face,
a slight curve of the lips,
and the ghost of laughter shared
resides in the chest.

Longing is too strong a word,
or too close to home maybe.
There is an ache in the heart
a tear balanced on the edge,
and the lie that love was not
holds prisoner this trust.

Kerri J. Roe

Batten Down

Swirling, howling, blasting
the wind beats at the door
Shutters shudder, clinging
to their perch, and
door holds the line
while chill infiltrates
the weak spots where
seals just can't hold out
Windows withstand the onslaught
though their groans slip
between their panes
And in the dark,
fading certainty
trembling bravado
and the fearful hollow
where confidence once
had flamed

Overlook

Scalding depths
of bathtub waves
sing of the peace
my body craves
Stars alight
through window glazed
belie the real
that days are crazed
The hopes atoss
the plans awry
and catching all these
tears denied
The burn of touch
upon my skin
now just a dream
the world locked in.

Kerri J. Roe

Untitled

The winter of your discontent
can never dam
the spring of my eternal hope

Icebound

crystalline hide
coated in frosted fur;
frozen shroud
fragile and hard.
veining fissures
cast faceted windows
on a snow globe world
where hope dances
in timid revelry.
half-dreamed wishes,
butterfly-winged love
flutter haltingly
in the icy shell
of a winter heart.

Riding The Rails

You look thinner
  hair unkempt
  clothes unwashed
I ask how you're doing
  where are you staying
  do you have food
You smile vaguely
  doesn't reach your eyes
  eyes that avoid mine
You say you're good
  got an okay place
  got big plans
I ask if you're eating
  offer a lunch date
  maybe some groceries
Ask about extracurriculars
  simple code for
  are you using

Kerri J. Roe

Tell you I'm worried
  offer help as I
  [secretly] scan for signs
You wear long sleeves
  pants that once fit
  taped-up shoes
Are you covering tracks?
  red eyes lacking sleep?
  are these gifts yours to give?
I watch, and I fear, and I
  tell you.

Tell you I love you too.

We both know
  I'm stupid
Both know I question
  your stories

My Heart Walks in Pieces

Both know I want you
  off
  this train you've boarded
Helpless as I try
  to show you
  hope
To show you
  love
To try to bring you back
  from the broken track.

But I am not the engineer,

And I fear
  you

are no longer

driving this train.

Kerri J. Roe

Prison Break

The door is open,
   I must escape
There is no time,
   it cannot wait
Must leave this cage
   of pens and files
where blood is spilt
   in red-tape miles
Duck under threat
   of deadline siege
and outrun duty's
   ravenous needs
Break free from
   tightened daily chains
expectation's gnawing
   strain
I must run free where

Nature Reigns

And stretch out with my
   arms flung wide
where breath can
   truly breathe

I must look far at tops of trees
   and mountain peaks
   and wild things
hear the calls of birds
   and streams

My Heart Walks in Pieces

taste the fresh
   in evergreen breeze
inhale heavy
   mossy scents
as ancient rumbled
   dirt is spent
   in lines between
   my toes

The lure of green
   and brown and blue
and all the rainbow's
   many hues
hails with need
   I can't refuse
There is no time,
   it cannot wait
for in the wilds
my heart awaits.

Kerri J. Roe

Awakening

And then the growth
started

No more of the bated
breath, waiting
for something

that never became.
No more of the holding
back, hoping
for rescue

that never came.
It started
with a small
shift, lifting
the heart

from its hiding place;
With a quiet
recognition
the soul

is a precious thing,
A sudden ancient
knowing
the worth of

the person within;
And then,

My Heart Walks in Pieces

a raise of
the head, a
straightening of
the shoulders, as
The strength of

one's being
spread its wings

and took flight

Kerri J. Roe

Nocturne's Spell

Daytimers don't know
how the night
becomes a magical place
how the meadow shines
in its secret way
when the moon traces
her fingers on the snow

They've never stood
grinning up in delight
at scattered stars
gazing back from deepest skies,
nor watched the
world
become
a faery place
with silver leaves
and lucent boughs
and creatures stirring
in the shadows

They don't long for
Luna's sweet caress, nor
for Selene's gentle breeze,
never fall yielding to
the allure of the gloaming's
whispered mysteries

My Heart Walks in Pieces

They don't feel
the cool hand of Eve
touch their cheeks
nor hear the songs of galaxies
drifting down in chimes
of star beams and moon shine
and Aurora's dancing
luminosity

Daytimers don't know
how the night
becomes a wondrous place
They don't know
the adoration of
the beauty
of the night

Kerri J. Roe

Beauty In the Dying

Lacy lines in frost
in curling leaf,
in this, her
paling face
The gray peers out
from colors
applied, an
artistry betraying
the battles fought
and the never-presented
decorations
of a life soldier

A map of blue
and purple
veins tangled
intersections on her
hands, trails along
arms and legs
and feet

Fluttering lash,
lover's voice
summons recollection
as she stands on
the threshold
where he cannot carry

My Heart Walks in Pieces

And in her newly
clear vision
the current of
their tears
washes away
leagues, and their
ships shelter together
in a harbor
of memory and grief.

Kerri J. Roe

Limbo

The soft hiss of oxygen
underlines
furtive whispers,
talk of wills and bills and probate
punctuated by
sporadically yelled words for
the hard-of-hearing patient,
delirium melding with dream-states
interspersed with clarity
that births false hope
of defeating fate inevitable.

That Moment

That moment when you stop to take a breath. When you feel the laughter about to burst from your chest. Where you drink in the beauty around you, or when you feel the love in every particle of your being. When peace settles over you with a welcoming sigh, holding you, for just a while, in its gentle embrace. *That* moment. Hold onto it, melt into it, revel in it, cherish it. Breathe deep of the strength within. Carry on, keeping this treasure safe within your heart, beating to the rhythms of the earth: You are loved. You are loved. You are loved. Let its glow be a light in the darkness.

Kerri J. Roe

Sylvan Shower

The torpedo call of the jay
Rat-a-tat of squirrel chatter
And staccato woodpecker beats
Padding cat feet on damp ground
Shy drops of a light rain
Dance on millions of leaves
Kissing upturned blushing faces
Of wild roses and honeysuckle
Lupine standing enrobed in royal shades
With crowns glowing white
Dandelions grown spiky in self-defense
Lest they lose their heads in the shower
Like the sparrows spinning dizzily
Heedless of the stern gaze of the spruce
And the whispered laughter of the birch
And the wallflower wishes of
The wanderer in the woods

G[r]o[w]ing

Distance measures out in
  mountains and pebbles
    and ocean waves
Heights stretching through
  peaks and treetops
   and fingers of flower petals
 reaching for one last bit
  of sunshine
 like roots searching ever
   deeper in loamy soil
   tasting every possible
  drop of sustenance
 tendrils spread as
moonbeams and starlight
   across the heavy
  expanse of night
   through the thick
        blanket of losing

 - I look at the stars and wonder,
  which will you be?

Passage

(for Grandpa)

How does one come to this?
Child of the woods,
Running, leaping, hunting, fishing
Self-sufficient from early days
Sleeping in the open
Since four years old
So much knowledge
Wisdom gained
Skills passed on

Eight decades plus
Of independence
And contriving
And economy
Respect for the hunted
Love for the weaker

And food set out
For small creatures.

My Heart Walks in Pieces

How does one come to this?
Entrapped by walls,
Groaning, cursing, mumbling, stuck
Pained dependence these later days
Sleeping in stealthy fits
Eighty-four years old
Jumbled knowledge
Wisdom fogged
Skills confounded

Chronos counts in days
Of helplessness
And painfulness
And expense
Afraid as the hunted
Ashamed to be weaker

And food set out
For small creatures.

Kerri J. Roe

Dreamscape

Streams of fallen tears flow over
Rocks polished smooth by
Timeworn memory
Watering the land of
Past, present, and future,
Banks covered with
Flowers of hope
Blooms of wishes
As clouds of dreams
Pass over in
An infinite sky.

Moonshine

Moonshine
Cool and perfect
On fallen snow
Starbright
Reflecting in crystals
No hand has known
Hushabye
Whispered in branches
Heavy-laden and low
Nightlife
In echoes of
This wilderness home

Kerri J. Roe

Epitaph

When I die,
Shed tears if you must
Let them wash
The scales from your eyes
Reveal the light
See all the little
Hidden things
That make the world beautiful

When I'm gone
Shout and wail if it helps
Let it crescendo
Into songs of life and movement
Raise your arms
Free your feet in

Dances
To secret music
That lifts the soul
Irresistibly

When I pass
Grow though the grief
Let it teach you to

Cherish

Moments
Lay bare your heart
Act with kindness

Let love live as my legacy

Breathing

Metamorphosis

Soft and pliant
No shield
No boundaries
No protections
Now hidden, now enwrapped
As a being ensorcelled
Cocooned in layers
A chrysalis of experiences
Of losses
And breakings
And shatterings
Now emerging, now changed
A creature unexpected
Broken from layers
A freedom of scars
- They didn't warn of the pain.

Kerri J. Roe

My Heart Walks in Pieces

Fragments scatter across the earth
Blown by wayward winds
And sudden leave-takings
And growing pains

Umbilical cords stretched taut
Twisted and wrenched
Tethered to this bruised heart
Unbreakably broken

Shuttered windows and locking doors
Pushed every limit
Right to the razor's edge
Yet this one remains open

Adventuring souls stake their flags
Claiming space for their dreams
And independences
And individuality

Winter brings refurbished wisdom
Fed by hunger and struggle
And knowledge of constancy
Shattered unbroken

My Heart Walks in Pieces

Leaves turning life's pirouette
Whispered almost-regrets
Prodigals return again
For love never left

Le Café

all alone
as she sits in the corner
steam rising from a cup
like the
conversations swirling through the air,
weaving around and past
invisible fences,
marking the spaces
that don't fit
and the holes unfilled.
music lifts with gentle caress,
notes of friendship
and melodies of memories
soothing storms hidden;
invisible worlds and tidepool dreams,
reveries of ethereal visions
ephemeral shadows behind her eyes,
like the
steam rising from a cup
as she sits in the corner
all alone.

Vignette

laying down the lines
borders and edges and form
smudging away the harshness
depth of shadow and movement
curve of cheek, curve of lip
hair blown by intangible breeze
emotion's flood brought forth
come to life on
bleached wood pulp
canvas's texture
invisible beauty
released through the
magic of her hands

Kerri J. Roe

River

You pass by,
liquid grace
power incarnate
Clothed in shades
of blues and greens and grays
Singing songs of distance
and place
Of time inexorable
immemorial
implacable
Speaking in tongues
language of the depths
and the depths of the soul
Instinctive
Unfettered
Whispering secrets and
dreams and
origins of legends
Carrying life in
the womb of your current
in your aqueous marrow
And holding peace
in the mesmerizing torrent
of your ferocious serenity

On the Backs of Waves

The whisper comes to me,
riding on the backs of waves
in a glassy sea as the light
appears in the distance,
a sign of hope under heavy clouds
a reminder that distance is only
a moment and the darkness
only momentary
And my heart, though scarred,
hears the Truth and recalls
that Poets
and Dreamers
are idealists,
gifts birthed in reverie,
in hope and
airy harmony,
and they must rest
within the Light.

Kerri J. Roe

The Artist

Deep in thought she sits
Listening to poets and singers
Cast their dreams,
Like cottonwood fluff
Coasting on breezes
In search of good soil
To take root
And stretch
In new directions;
Hopes and sorrows
Dressed as words and notes,
Full and robust yet
Clothed in nervous trust
And she fills the snowdrifts
Of her paper with lines
And colors, putting form
To the heartsongs and soul dreams
Suspended in the air

Reflections

Reflections
Of mountains
Deep, ponderous thoughts
Grounded in centuries of folding
and building
and carving of
Water
As glacier
in frozen sculptor's tools
shaping, uncovering long-hidden truths
As rivers
fast white-water dreams,
began with gurgling brooks
and ending
and resting
in calm quiet lakes
surrounded by
Forests
Ancient spires
New spring greens giving way to
Decadent summer foliage
Inhabited by creatures
come to drink
to find sustenance
perhaps unaware in the water
echoes their beauty, their woodlands,
their mountains
in calmness, in quietness,
these silent
Reflections

Kerri J. Roe

A Legacy in Crystal

The glow of warm lights
wraps its arms around
traveler and couple
and quiet dreamer
gazing out
at the flurries, the
same in their shade
and in their cold
and in their errant,
erratic, swirling descent
toward frozen ground

The variety of their paths
a feast to those who look,
intricacies of their individual
shapes noted by the dedicated
and the patient and the
ones who look deep,
infinitely different,

Infinitely beautiful,
each one a fingerprint
of its own faithful
hopes, dreams of
drift or tree-lace
or child's laughing
snowball-fight screams

Evidence of their
numbers piling up
in hills and cakes, covering

My Heart Walks in Pieces

roofs and transforming
landscapes into a
new sort of world
where the magic
of wonder and the
power of love

illuminate
the darkness,
where hearts hold
no malice,
where brother
recognizes brother,
no matter his shape
no matter his shade

Snowflakes dancing,
drifting, bumping
their way through a life of
indescribable
Beauty and
unpredictable winds,
and the shapes we make
as we come together
become
the picture of our legacy
before our bodies
melt into the land

Kerri J. Roe

Sway

Suspended
in the sound of leaves
mimicking water's hushed
rush under the
chee-chee-hee-hee of
goshawks and sparrows
countered by a duck's
scolding call

Dry yellow grass
interrupted in its plodding
monologue by the
impudence of green
upstarts stretching towards
evening's golden light

Whistling songs alight on
the breeze as stripey things
buzz around blossoms
and petals soaking up
summer's short shining

Tall grasses who haven't met
this year's mower dance
freedom of unbridled growth
and the trees burst forth
in songbirds of laughter
leaves tickling their
parchment-paper bark

My Heart Walks in Pieces

Coaxing them out of
deep-rooted wonderings
to play chase with the
day's shadows
and rock-a-bye
lullaby in the
slumbers
of the
night

Kerri J. Roe

Apini

Striped friend, what do you think
                 As you flit about your business,
Tasting and touching and carrying
       Your inadvertent treasure of
            Gold from bud to blossom?
   Do your wings tire
Of hovering, endlessly moving,
                Breaking laws of physics
   And gravity and urbanity,
      A rebel without intention?

   Do you have a favorite
            Flavor of flower,
  A dish you prefer
       Of rosebud or lilac
     Or some exotic bloom
             Served in a gourmet garden?
   Do you wonder which petal

          Will be the sweetest
  Or long for meadows where
      Greener grass lies on all sides?

Bounty

Tiny worlds in rainbow hues
hide in depths of jewel-
toned leaves, in the
burning shades of frost-
seared fall, the damp
air a near-welcome
touch, the rustle of breeze-
tossed foliage interrupted
by the crunch of steps
in fallen brethren, the
scent of their released breath
a sweet prelude inhaled,
skins bursting as their
nectar fills eager mouth
slides over tongue
and chin and stained
kaleidoscope fingers

Kerri J. Roe

Gossamer

Charcoal clouds scud across
an ocean of sky,
a thread of song running
counterpoint to
the pictures in my mind
an unintended soundtrack
rising and falling
to a disparate rhythm,
now background, now cacophony
full of its own words
stories to tell in notes
and tunes and cymbals clashing
as I fall deeper in
like Alice,
into imagination
and dream-worlds
and the realities of
make-believe
until a warm touch
on my shoulder
brings me out of my reveries
waking to the sun's caress
reaching through aged clouds
bidding me arise, awake,

My Heart Walks in Pieces

return from the land of
mushroom rings and
flaming kings and
queens of beauty bright;

Disconcerted,
I raise my head,
blink in unexpected light
summoned from
my home

to this strange and
Earthly life.

Kerri J. Roe

Water, Living

Brilliance
of diamonds
gemstones formed
in sliding droplets
reflecting the light
revealing the nature
of things
with unparalleled

clarity

silent
crystal balls
in millions innumerable
magnifying the present
portending a future they
nourish
creating their own

destiny

in absorption into
laughing loving leaves
and reaching, thirsty
souls

Oculus

Oh, I could sing to you
  of the moon on frost-feathered
    branches
  and the music that plays
    in the night
  of the bright stars' dark deep
    lullaby
  and how the mist breezes
    sigh
I could teach to you
  lissome fairies' dance
    steps
  and the constellations' rock-steady
    guide
  the secrets of leafy forest
    pathways
  and the language of ocean's
    goodbyes
I could hold out this world
  in my heart to you
  but you hold my heart
    in your eyes

Kerri J. Roe

That Thing with Feathers

Hope
is a thing with feathers,
or so the poet wrote
It beats against the breast
fighting its way against
the cage of caution and
hard lessons and
regret
Hope is an untameable
creature slipping between bars
too weak to hold it captive
It lifts and dips and whirls
following updrafts of
possibilities
In dreams and whispers
and wistful wishes
Hope is the thing with power
to rise and Rise again
to overcome and conquer
It holds the line
refusing retreat from
the threat of disappointment
and cynicism and despair

My Heart Walks in Pieces

Hope is the Savior
and the Victor
The Hero of Love,
the Merciful Touch,
and Rescue of the lost
Hope is the lighthouse beacon,
the joyful freedom
Hope is the Light in the dark.

Kerri J. Roe

Breathe

Breathe
Breathe in me
Your stillness, your quiet
Breathe in me
Your peace
Your hope
Your love so unbelievably deep

Breathe
Spill your laughter
Into my soul
So that it
Spills out of my lungs
Bubbling up in joy
And smiles
And moments of contentment

Breathe in me
The life you meant
For me to live
Whisper away
My fears and insecurities
Still the nervous
Echo of my heart
And the worries writhing in my veins

Breathe
Like the breeze in trees
Air currents on water

My Heart Walks in Pieces

Breath that gives life
And words
And dreams
And peace

Breathe.

With Immeasurable Thanks

First to you, dear readers, for taking the time to read some of my words. I am honored by your trust and hope they have touched your heart in some bright way. Thanks to the women of Writers Anonymous, who have helped me find my voice in ink and in life over the course of two decades and who've seen these poems in several forms. To my ARC readers, especially K. Lorentzen and SethWilson Gray, for invaluable feedback. To my family, for putting up with my love-need relationship with writing—words can never say how much you mean to me. And to Friðrik, for encouraging and supporting me in my many, many, (did I say many?) projects: thank you for loving me so well. I love every one of you.

About The Author

Kerri J. Roe is a multi-genre writer with publications in *Cirque*, *Alaska Women Speak*, and the anthology *Feisty Felines and Other Fantastic Familiars*. She is a 2024 AWP Intro Awards Nominee in poetry. She holds degrees in English, Psychology, and Counselor Education, and is a candidate for the MFA in Creative Writing at Mississippi University for Women. Kerri lives with her family in the Pacific Northwest, obsessing over books, eating chocolate, and being enticed by the magic of nature.

Learn more at kerrijroe.com

Instagram @bookkerri
Facebook Kerri J. Roe, Writer
TikTok and X @kerrijroe

Kerri J. Roe

Acknowledgments

The following poems were previously published in Alaska Women Speak under the name KJ Roe:
Dreamscape – Fall 2016
Icebound – Winter 2016
Passion – Summer 2017

The following poems have appeared on the author's earlier blog, www.dreamsofshadowandlight.wordpress.com and on the Facebook page by the same name:

Deafening
Drops of Time
Elemental
From the Ashes
Gossamer
Jericho
Le Café
Limbo
Metamorphosis
Nebula
Passage
Precipitous
Reflections
Riding the Rails
River
Sylvan Shower
Tesserae
The Artist
Voice

Thoughts & Musings

Kerri J. Roe

May you go forth with the
light of love on your face
the glow of peace in your mind
and the seed of hope in your heart.

www.ingramcontent.com/pod-product-compliance
Lightning Source LLC
Chambersburg PA
CBHW020556030426
42337CB00013B/1117